Forever and Ever

by
Kathleen H. Barnes
Virginia H. Pearce

Photographs by
Don O. Thorpe

A Book for LDS Children about
Temple Marriage

Published by Deseret Book Company
Salt Lake City, Utah
1975

Copyright © 1975
by
Deseret Book Company

Library of Congress Catalog Card No. 75-28899
ISBN 0-87747-603-9

Printed in the United States of America

What therefore God hath joined together, let not man put asunder. (Mark 10:9.)

Today Alice and Paul are getting married forever and ever and ever.

Everyone has been so busy.
Mother has been sewing.
Daddy has been writing checks.
My big brother has a new haircut.
Alice is on a diet.
And I went to a grown-up party.

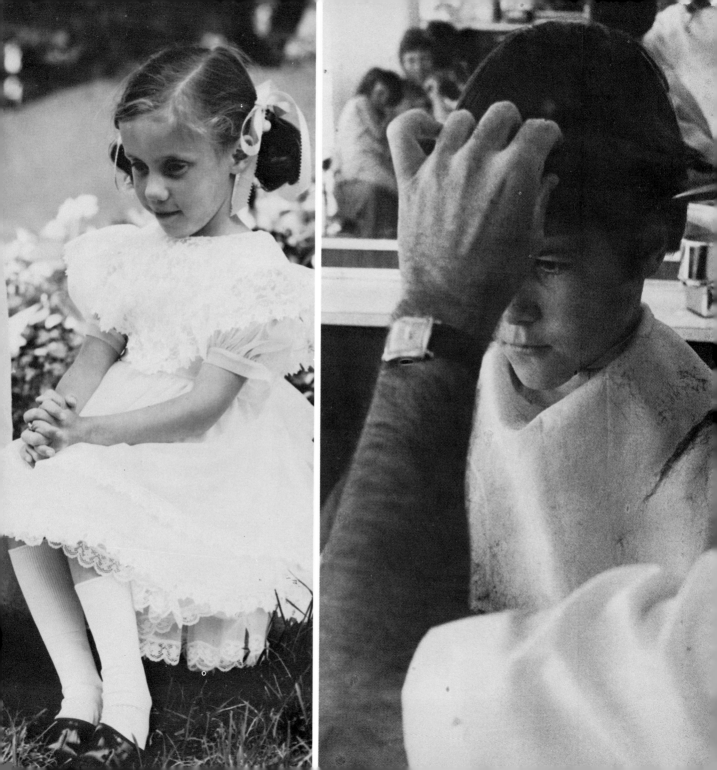

Big white packages with white bows have been arriving at the door for days. These are wedding gifts for Alice and Paul.

And now the big day is here. This morning we woke up very early and we all put on our best clothes.

On our way to the temple Mother said, "You and your big brother cannot go into the temple this morning, but you may wait on the grounds until we come out."

First we walked around the temple
and counted all the windows.
Then we jumped along the walk
without stepping on the lines.
It seemed like hours, but still
Alice and Paul didn't come out.

"Why are they taking so long?" I asked my brother. "And why can't we go in? What are they doing in there?" Then my big brother told me again what we had learned in family home evening about temple marriage.

He says that in the temple it is very quiet. First Alice and Paul go to special dressing rooms. They dress in beautiful white clothing. "I'll bet they look like angels," I say.

Alice and Paul walk down wide, quiet hallways and go into the marriage room. Mother and Daddy, Grandma and Grandpa, and other special people all sit in soft chairs.

...if a man marry a wife, and make a covenant with her for time and for all eternity, if that covenant is not by me...through him whom I have anointed and appointed unto this power, then it is not valid...
(D&C 132:18.)

Only men with special authority
can make Alice the wife
and Paul the husband –
forever.

Nevertheless neither is the man without the woman, neither the woman without the man, in the Lord. (1 Corinthians 11:11.)

Alice and Paul kneel at an altar,
Alice on one side, Paul on the other.
They make promises to each other
and to Heavenly Father. They
promise to love each other and to
love Heavenly Father always.
They promise to make their home
a happy and heavenly place.
And Heavenly Father promises
that they'll always be together
even after they leave this earth.

Therefore, if a man marry him a wife in the world, and he marr[y] her not by me nor by my word, and he covenant with her so long as h[e] is in the world and she with him, their covenant and marriage ar[e] not of force when they are dead....   (D&C 132:15[)]

My brother says that if they were not married in the temple, their promises would not be with Heavenly Father, and they would be together only for a time.

...and they shall pass by the angels, and the gods, which are set there, to their exaltation and glory in all things, as hath been sealed upon their heads, which glory shall be a fulness and a continuation of the seeds forever and ever. (D&C 132:19.)

When I get married, I might have grown-up parties and white packages with white bows. But I'm *sure* I want to be married in a temple and make promises that will last forever and ever and ever.

What therefore God hath joined together, let not man put asunder. (Mark 10:9.)